To My Pa

Praise God
work He has done in
us! Thank you for being pliable
in the Master's hands — for
without your yieldedness in
this long and tedious process,
we could not have reached
this place called "friendship."
Looking forward to the
manifestation of our divine
assignment come to fruition.

Love You! ♡
Valerie
12/2012

The Spiritual Demise of the Church

Carnality

Complacency

&

Compromise

By
Dr. Darlene Townsend

Covers Designed by Kingdom Printing

Printed in USA

Unless otherwise indicated, all Scripture quotations are taken from the *King James Version* of the Bible.

The Spiritual Demise of the Church –
Carnality, Complacency & Compromise

ISBN 1-4196-9973-3

Copyright © 2008 by Dr. Darlene Townsend
All Rights Reserved

No part of this book may be reproduced, stored in a retrieval system, or transmitted by any means without written permission from the author.

Printed in the United States of America

FOREWORD

If you are looking for a new dimension in your spiritual life, this is a must for you to read. *The Spiritual Demise of the Church* is a book that does not sugar-coat the truth, but stands on the biblical principles of God's word without compromise.

Dr. Townsend is sending out a wake-up call to the body of Christ about the deceptive devices of Satan. God is looking for vessels to cry aloud and spare not, and Dr. Townsend has done so in the pages of this book.

Knowledge is power; therefore after reading this book one can take a spiritual inventory of their life to make sure they are not missing the mark.

Darlene challenges you to rise above the obstacles that the body of Christ faces, and not allow yourself to become infested with carnality, complacency, and compromise. It is time for the body of Christ to take a stand for holiness and righteousness.

This book is, without question, a spiritual makeover for the body of Christ. Darlene has a unique talent for making deep spiritual concepts immediately accessible. With *The Spiritual Demise of the Church*, she has hit a homerun!

I am certain if you follow the principles laid out in this book, you will not become a victim of the tactics that the enemy has set up for the believers, but you will become an example of the true representation of God's word – for we are God's living epistles.

As you read Dr. Townsend's book, I hope you will be obedient to join her in the pursuit of bringing back into the body of Christ a spirit of integrity, truth, and deliverance so that the manifestation of God can be seen.

– Dr. John H. Boyd, Sr.

DEDICATED TO

The remnant in the body of Christ
Who truly hunger and thirst after
righteousness –
Who have a made up mind to serve Christ
and not their flesh –
Who are sick and tired of playing "church" –
Who are ready to *"Enter ye in at the strait gate: for wide is the gate, and broad is the way, that leadeth to destruction, and many there be which go in thereat:*
Because strait is the gate, and narrow is the way, which leadeth unto life,
and few there be that find it."
Matthew 7:13, 14

ACKNOWLEDGEMENTS

Rev. Elaine Lee
The first person to speak these words into
the atmosphere and into my spirit –
"Get this published!"
Thank you.

Tallie Gainer, III
For your priceless words of
encouragement, your spirit of
perseverance, your faithfulness in guiding
my vision, and your refusal to accept
anything contrary to making this happen!
Thank you.

The Holy Spirit
Who planted this seed, watered it, and
gives it the ultimate increase –
For this, I am forever grateful for
your impartation of
wisdom, knowledge, and grace.
Thank you.

TABLE OF CONTENTS

                              Page

INTRODUCTION............................ 1

CHAPTER ONE:
THE LAODICEAN ERA............... 10

CHAPTER TWO:
THE WAY OF
HOLINESS................................ 21

CHAPTER THREE:
THE CHURCH EXPOSED 31

CHAPTER FOUR:
THE CHRISTIAN VOICE –
THE SURVEY 58

CONCLUSION 80

BIBLIOGRAPHY 85

INTRODUCTION

Since the beginning of time, mankind has succumbed to its sinful nature in spite of the severity of its consequences. Throughout the Holy Scriptures, believers are repeatedly admonished to ... "abstain from the sensual urges (the evil desires, the passions of the flesh, your lower nature) that wage war against the soul" (1 Peter 2:11 AMP).

The believer must recognize that there is a war going on – a spiritual battle between the forces of darkness and God's angelic beings. The enemy fights to gain control over the mind and flesh in an attempt to win the soul. This spiritual conflict will continue throughout one's lifetime so the believer must gird up with the spiritual weapons and armor recorded in Ephesians 6:12-18. Even though this battle is not necessarily fought in the physical realm, it is truly a matter of life and death.

This book will make you raise your consciousness to the debilitating spiritual state of the church. The leaders of the church are: diluting the gospel with promises of prosperity without the application of Godly principles; preaching and teaching God's Word, but living another – bearing the decaying fruit of carnality, complacency, and compromise. _Webster's II New College Dictionary_, defines these abominable fruits in the following manner:

> Carnal – relating to sensual desires and appetites; earthly: temporal.
>
> Complacency – satisfaction or contentment.
>
> Compromise – a settlement of differences in which each side makes concessions. Something combing qualities of two different things. A concession to something that is harmful or depreciative. [1]

This book will demonstrate how sin separates man from God and that God will continue to expose leaders and laymen alike for their disobedience. God is true to His Word, "For the time is come that judgment must begin

---

[1] _Webster's II New College Dictionary_, (Boston, MA: Houghton Mifflin Company, 2001), pp. 169, 229.

at the house of God: and if it first begin at us, what shall the end be of them that obey not the gospel of God?" (1Peter 4:17). If the saints of God fail to live according to the Word of God, how will sinners or even backsliders desire to enter the household of faith? Although all men are drawn unto God by the Holy Spirit, where will they go to be fed the spiritual food for survival in this wicked world? "For whosoever shall call upon the name of the Lord shall be saved. How then shall they call on him in whom they have not believed? and how shall they hear without a preacher? And how shall they preach, except they be sent? ..." (Romans 10:13-15).

While death is not a choice topic for discussion, it is necessary to highlight some relevant points to enhance your understanding of this phenomenon. Death can occur in three different phases: 1) physical 2) spiritual and 3) eternal. **Physical death** is the cessation of all physiological functions (e.g., breathing, heart rate, etc.) in the body. At that precise moment, the soul and spirit are separated from the body, whether one is a believer or not. **Spiritual death** (or demise) is the state of the unregenerate man who is unsaved or destitute of salvation. <u>The New Bible Dictionary</u>, edited by I. Howard Marshall, et al comments on spiritual death as:

> That more serious death is the divine penalty...We are not caught up in a web woven by blind fate, so that, once having sinned, nothing can ever be done about it. God is over the whole process, and, if he has decreed that death is the

penalty of sin, he has also determined to give life eternal to those saved by Christ.[2]

Eternal death is the eternal separation from God in a conscious state of suffering. This death will occur at The Great White Throne Judgment where the unsaved and hell will be cast into the lake of fire, as noted in the book of Revelation 20:11-15.

Immorality in the church is not a new phenomenon, neither has it lost its fervor nor momentum over the centuries. Interestingly, we currently live in an age where more and more Christians are being educated about the Word of God through various teaching methods such as

---

[2] I. Howard Marshall, A.R. Millard, J.I. Packer and D.J. Wiseman, *The New Bible Dictionary*, (Downers Grove, Illinois: Intervarsity Press, 1999), pp. 265, 266.

organized Bible studies, correspondence courses, certificate, and degree programs. It has become very popular to attend local and national conferences, seminars, and workshops of prominent televangelists, preachers, teachers, and prophets. If you cannot attend an event, videotapes, cassette tapes, and DVDs are made available for purchase via mail or electronic mail (email) for spiritual edification. Hosea 4:6 reads, *"My people are destroyed for lack of knowledge: because thou hast **rejected** knowledge, I will also reject thee, that thou shalt be no priest to me..."*

With the abundance of biblical, spiritual, and inspirational tools accessible today for hearing the Word of God, believers are more accountable for living and abiding in the truth of the Holy Scriptures than ever before.

In divine sequential order, the Bible identifies various events that will occur and prophetically declares the end-times. The Bible speaks of wars and rumors of wars, famines, pestilence, earthquakes, and false prophets rising up (Matthew 24:5-7, 11). Believers can no longer afford to merely be *hearers* of the word only, and *not doers.* Living in these perilous times, the enemy will subtly snuff the Spirit of God from the believer if you remain carnal, complacent, and compromising God's standard of living while seeking temporary self-gratification, leading to your spiritual demise.

"...Woe to the inhabiters of the earth and of the sea! For the devil is come down unto you having great wrath, because he knoweth that he hath but a short time."
(Revelation 12:12 KJV)

CHAPTER ONE

THE LAODICEAN ERA

"I know thy works, that thou are neither cold not hot: I would thou wert cold or hot. So then because thou art lukewarm, and neither cold nor hot, I will spue thee out of my mouth. Because thou sayest, I am rich, and increased with goods, and have need of nothing; and knowest not that thou are wretched, and miserable, and poor, and blind, and naked. . . As many as I love, I rebuke and chasten: be zealous therefore and repent."
Revelation 3:15-17, 19 (KJV)

Throughout the past few decades, the signs of the times have revealed a vast falling away of members from the body of Christ, particularly its leaders. Today, many believers have adopted the "lukewarm" mentality of the Laodicean church. John Walvoord states in his book, *The Revelation of Jesus Christ*, that:

> ...*lukewarmness* is what characterized the church in Laodicea. This state refers to those who have manifested some interest in the things of God. They may be professing Christians who attend church but have fallen far short of a true testimony for Christ and whose attitude and actions raise questions concerning the reality of their spiritual life. They have been touched by the gospel, but it is not clear whether they really belong to Christ.[3]

"The city of Laodicea was founded by Antiochus II in the middle of the third century before Christ and named after his wife, Laodice. It was situated about forty miles southeast of

---

[3] John F. Walvoord, *The Revelation of Jesus Christ*, (Chicago, IL: Moody Press, 1989) p. 92.

Philadelphia on the road to Colossae."[4] Accordingly, the author John Walvoord gives you additional insight into the occurrences at the church in Laodicea, which states:

> When destroyed by an earthquake about A.D. 60, it was able to rebuild without any outside help. Its economic sufficiency tended to lull the church to sleep spiritually; and though there is mention of the church as late as the fourteenth century, the city as well as the church now is in complete ruins.[5]

According to the *Laodicea txt*, "The citizens of Laodicea were the wealthiest in the metropolis of Asia Minor as a result of their production of a high-grade black glossy wool (resembling silk); a school of medicine that formulated the eye salve to cure weak eyes

---
[4] *Ibid.* p. 89.
[5] John Walvoord, p. 89.

which was exported in tablet form throughout the Mediterranean; and considered 'the' banking center of the metropolis."[6] Similar to the Laodiceans, believers today are concerned with earning higher wages; better working conditions (as evidenced by unions and labor laws); better housing conditions and good physical health.

The Laodiceans were also full of pride as evidenced in the Scripture stating that they had "need of nothing." The Lord does not rebuke any of the other seven churches in book of Revelation like this church. God cannot stomach a believer who is lukewarm and requires that one take a stand – hot or cold. The Spirit of the Lord speaks of the monetary

---

[6] "Laodicea txt.www.ourfatherlutheran.net

increase of these people yet, He accuses them of being "wretched, miserable, poor, blind, and naked" because they lacked spiritual revelation of Him.

The church in Laodicea boasted of its material wealth, while lacking spiritual perception, devotion, and faith in God, which ultimately made them poor. Their primary focus was the acquisition of wealth and being self-sufficient. This is deception, a trick from the enemy because no one can depend on "self" and please God. Proverbs 3:5,6 reads, "Trust in the LORD with all thine heart; and lean not unto thine own understanding. In all thy ways acknowledge him, and he shall direct thy paths." With the natural eye, it appears that the

Laodiceans were successful people. However, Walvoord further tells us that:

> The church at Laodicea with their unconscious need were lulled into *false contentment* by their *temporal sufficiency*. Spiritually they were in a wretched state but did not realize it. Without the real joy of the Lord, they were miserable in spite of their temporal wealth. They were poor because they were without real and eternal possessions...[7]

The commonalities found between the Laodiceans and the Christian church today is the spirit of pride, haughtiness, idolatry, and the love of money. The Christian church exudes with the spirit of pride and haughtiness as evidenced by the incessant preaching and teaching on prosperity. The primary focus of the church is acquiring wealth. Ministries have

---
[7] Walvoord, p. 94.

developed creative tactics, movements, partnerships, and crusades to raise large offerings (e.g., $50, $100, $1000, etc.); increasing church memberships verses saving souls; and building grandiose church edifices.

The spirit of competition has also manifested in the body of Christ, whereby members are preoccupied with status, titles, positions, and recognition predominantly within the five-fold ministry. Additionally, Christians are investing more in dressing up their outward appearances and neglecting the inward appearances. Matthew 6:21 clearly states, "For where your treasure is, there will your heart be also."

The Christian church today is proud to send its leaders to mount great platforms and fill stadiums with thousands and thousands of people with television and print media coverage as well as the opportunity to sell thousands of dollars worth of merchandise, and receive national acclaim. While it is God's will that His people "...prosper and be in good health..." (3 John 2), it is not the heartbeat of the gospel. God sent His Son, Jesus, to give His life for the sinner that one may have eternal life. Jesus came to save, heal, deliver, and set the captives free.

Like the Laodiceans, the Christian church is also controlled by the spirit of idolatry. Although statutes of gods are not physically erected in the church, these idols are monuments within the hearts of the believers and manifested in various channels of communication (e.g., daily conversations, speeches, sermons, etc.). These observations concur with Matthew 12:34, "...for out of the abundance of the heart the mouth speaketh."

The love of money is a dangerous and compromising state for the believer because it causes one to err from the faith and jeopardizes a right relationship with God. The Apostle Paul informs the reader in the Amplified version of 1 Timothy 6:10, "For the love of money is a root of all evils; it is through this craving that some have been led astray and have wandered from the faith and pierced themselves through with many acute [mental] pangs."

The spirit of pride, haughtiness, and idolatry is a malignancy that is rapidly spreading throughout the members of the body of Christ in epidemic proportions. The church body is more concerned about buying the new house (preferably in a gated community) in the suburbs with a four car garage; the Mercedes Benz or a fully loaded Escalade SUV; membership at the popular country club; a wardrobe with the latest exquisite fashions; investments and bank accounts with at least six digit figures. While all these material things can be a blessing, they can also be a curse. If these blessings hinder your spiritual growth and desensitize your spiritual consciousness, you will find yourself neglecting to seek the Lord in all things.

More importantly, believers must repent to receive the blessings of the Lord and escape eternal damnation. God loves His children; however, he will rebuke and chasten those that go astray from His will.

The Christian church no longer has the luxury of basking in its *lukewarm* state of mind because the stakes are too high. *It is truly a matter of life or death!*

CHAPTER TWO

THE WAY OF HOLINESS

*"And an highway shall be there, and a way, and it shall be called
The way of holiness; the unclean shall not pass over it; but it shall be for those: the wayfaring men, though fools, shall not err therein."*
Isaiah 35:8 (KJV)

Unfortunately, there are Christians that believe that living "holy" is unattainable; that mankind is merely human. Some of the common excuses that believers give for not living holy include, but are not limited to: "I can't"; "I don't want to"; "I'm only human"; "I'm not a nun"; "Only God is holy"; "God does not expect me to be perfect"; "It's too difficult"; and "It's virtually impossible to live holy in this evil world."

For the Christian, "the way of holiness is a walk of faith and obedience in the life of progressive sanctification made possible in us by the Holy Spirit through obedience to the Word of God."[8] Holiness is evident in the life of a Christian when we are totally devoted to God, set aside for His sacred use, and set apart from sin and its influence.

---

[8] Stephen F. Olford, *The Way of Holiness*, (Wheaton, Illinois: Good News Publishers, 1998), p. 9.

The Revel Bible Dictionary defines "holy", "holiness" as:

> (1) God himself in his essential nature; (2) persons, places, things, and times set apart or consecrated to God and therefore sacred; (3) a quality of character and actions that is in harmony with God's nature and expressed will.[9]

It can be surmised that believers stray away from living "holy" for the following reasons: a conscious and rebellious mindset; inadequate, improper or lack of teaching of biblical truths by church leadership; the inability to witness by example other believers living holy; and being ignorant of the Word of God. While God is merciful, He will not change His Word to accommodate the frailties of mankind.

---

[9] *The Revell Bible Dictionary*, (Grand Rapids, MI: Baker Book House Company, 1994), pp. 488, 489.

Christians must come to the realization that living holy is *not* an option, but rather a calling. The Holy Scriptures clearly state, "For God hath not called us unto uncleanness, but unto holiness" (1 Thessalonians 4:7). If one is identified as a believer, a child of God, then that child should take on the purity of His Heavenly Father's character - holiness. The Amplified text of 1 Peter 1:15, 16 reads, "But as the One Who called you is holy, you yourselves also be holy in all your conduct and manner of living. Because it is written, Be ye holy; for I am holy." God justifies the person who sins through salvation and declares you holy through the blood of Jesus. It is *only* through the blood of Jesus that believers are considered holy in the sight of the Holy God because all of man's good works are like filthy rags.

There are numerous references in the Old Testament and New Testament that decree the standards of holiness set by God as well as His expectations for His people to live accordingly. In the Old Testament, God demanded His people to live holy in the following manner: external or ceremonial and internal, or moral and spiritual.[10] The New Testament focuses primarily on "inner holiness" which is guided through and by the power and work of the Holy Spirit in the believer. Since the Holy Spirit comes from God, the Spirit shows the

---

[10] *Ilumina Encyclopedia*, (CD-ROM:Tyndale House Publishers, 2002).

believer God's holy character and accomplishes God's holy purposes in the world.[11]

The Way of Holiness by Stephen F. Olford, highlights eight *signposts* that believers can utilize as a guide in their walk of holiness, which include: 1) Sinfulness 2) Forgiveness 3) Holiness 4) Christ-Centeredness 5) Yieldedness 6) Spirit-Fullness 7) Usefulness and 8) Readiness.[12] Due to the length of these topics, the writer is unable to cover all the signposts listed above. However, I recommend that you take the liberty of perusing these topics more thoroughly for your spiritual edification. As such,

---

[11] *Ilumina Encyclopedia*
[12] Stephen F. Olford, *The Way of Holiness*, (Wheaton, Illinois: Good News Publishers, 1998), pp. 47 – 56.

I draw your attention specifically to the "Signpost of Holiness".

Stephen F. Olford reiterates many of the points the writer has previously discussed on holiness. Interestingly, I view the attestation of scriptural holiness as twofold: 1) yieldedness to God and 2) fruitfulness for God.[13] Christians must be yielded to God so that He can manifest His holiness in their lives. The Bible reads "...Present your bodies a living sacrifice, holy, acceptable unto God, which is your reasonable service" and "...for as ye have yielded your members servants to uncleanness and to iniquity unto iniquity; even so now yield your members servants to righteousness unto

---

[13] *Ibid* .pp. 52 – 56.

holiness" (Romans 12:1; 6:19). The believer must understand that yielding and surrendering to God is a daily process. "But the word of the LORD was unto them precept upon precept, precept upon precept; line upon line, line upon line; here a little, and there a little..." (Isaiah 27:13).

Olford further asserts that fruitfulness for God is a by-product of yieldedness to God, which includes: Christian worship, (Hebrews 13:5, John 4:23, Proverbs 3:9); the Christian walk (John 15:8, Galatians 5:22-23); and Christian work (John 15:15, Romans 1:13, Hebrews 12:14).[14] In the book of Romans 6:22, it reads, "But now being made free from sin, and

---

[14] Stephen Olford, *The Way of Holiness*. pp. 53-56.

become servants to God, ye have your fruit unto holiness, and the end everlasting life."

Essentially, God sets the standard of holiness for the believer because He is holy. It is imperative that the believer understand that living holy cannot be achieved by merely concerning yourself with the outer appearance like the Pharisees (e.g., looking religious with a "holier than thou" attitude, seeking the praises and recognition of men rather than God, hypocritical, obedient to the law yet disobedient to the Word of God); as well as wearing long outer garments or apparel often associated with men and women of God. Without the indwelling power of the Holy Spirit operating in the believer, it is impossible to live holy because it requires covenant faithfulness and wholehearted obedience to God.

> ***...Holy, holy, holy, Lord God Almighty, which was, and is, and is to come.***
> (Revelation 4:8 KJV).

CHAPTER THREE

THE CHURCH EXPOSED

*Your nakedness will be exposed and your shame uncovered.
I will take vengeance; I will spare no one."*
(Isaiah 47:3 NIV)

Throughout church history, disorder in the church has not been eradicated in spite of extensive acquisition of biblical training and instruction by leadership in this current church era. Like the Corinthian church, the Christian church today is also filled with idolatry, disunity, deception, and sexual immorality. Apostle Paul also articulates the following for the Corinthian church: concern for divisions in the church; condemnation for disorder in the church; and recommends counsel for the difficulties in the church.[15] The Amplified version in 1 Corinthians 5:6 states, "[About the condition of your church] your boasting is not good [indeed, it is most unseemly and entirely out of place]. Do you not know that [just] a little leaven will ferment the whole lump [of dough]?" The Word of God admonishes the believer not to give place to the devil (Ephesians 4:2) and assures that Christians should not be ignorant of Satan's

---

[15] *The Open Bible Expanded Edition*, (Nashville, TN: Thomas Nelson Publishers, 1985), p. 1157.

devices (2 Corinthians 2:11). On the contrary, many believers have become puppets for Satan in his calculating and divisive schemes to destroy God's people. The enemy is merely on his post and fulfilling his mission which is to steal, kill, and destroy (John 10:10).

Too many saints of God are going to and fro, seeking to be men-pleasers rather than God-pleasers; seeking men to "open up doors" for ministry instead of God; seeking prestige and power without the Holy Ghost; sneaking and seeking to walk in the flesh and not in the Spirit; seeking another's anointing instead of receiving God's anointing; seeking a greater anointing without a greater price; seeking ministry without brokenness; seeking status and recognition instead of seeking God and His righteousness; seeking to mount large platforms to be honored by the masses without being honored by God; and seeking fame and fortune even if it means prostituting the gifts of the Holy Spirit at the expense of bleeding the body of Christ of finances.

The Christian church is being anesthetized by the ploys of the enemy into a slow spiritual death because carnality, complacency, and compromise have become all too familiar. As a result, it is becoming increasingly more difficult to discern the "saints" from the "aints". The sinner is virtually turned off by "church folk" because there are fewer and fewer differences observed between the two lifestyles. Sinners witness Christians bicker, backbite, lie, steal, curse, drink, fornicate, and carouse, to name a few. While Christians are not perfect, the church is yet viewed as a safe haven, a place of peace, love, and healing. If sinners feel they will be misused and abused by men and women of God by entering the doors of the church, then believers have lost the battle to win souls for Christ. Until men and women and of God yield to the Holy Spirit, repent to God, stop playing church, abort the Hollywood mentality and surrender personal agendas, many lost souls will remain that – lost.

The Tragedy of Carnality, Complacency, and Compromise

> *Put to death, therefore, whatever in you is earthly: fornication, impurity, passion, evil desire, and greed (which is idolatry). On account of these the wrath of God is coming on those who are disobedient.*
> (Colossians 3:5,6 NRSV)

Over the past few decades, there has been an alarming upsurge of media attention and adverse publicity exposing the sins of church leaders and televangelists. While all sin and fall short of the glory of God (Romans 3:23), Christians cannot become complacent in sin and expect an omniscient, yet merciful God to allow such behavior to continue without severe ramifications. Remember, God is a holy God who cannot tolerate sin. Furthermore, the prophet Isaiah in 9:16 declares, *"For the leaders of his people cause them to err; and they that are led of them are destroyed."*

In, <u>No God But God</u>, Guinness and Seel state:

> Whenever immortality becomes the central objective of an organization, its demise is inevitable. Concern for the self-perpetuation of the institution and the preservation of the status quo is the greatest idol that any institution will face.[16]

It is imperative that believers perform a self-evaluation of themselves and seek God's help to remove false imaginations that rises above God. According to Guinness and Seel, *"Evangelicals are falling victim to the worst sin against faith – idolizing the products of the 'imaginations of our hearts."* The believer must

---

[16] Os Guinness & John Seel, <u>No God But God</u>. (Chicago, Illinois: Zonderan Publishing House, 1992), p. 37.

be prayed up at all times because *"we are all prone to idols – good and useful things inflated as substitutes for God, compensating for our need for control and significance."*[17]

St. John 15:19 reads, *"If ye were of the world, the world would love his own; but because ye are not of the world, but I have chosen you out of the world, therefore the world hateth you."* Being a Christian and living Christ-like should not resemble or mimic the stench or appearance of rotten fruits in this world. When a believer's lifestyle crosses over the line of Godly principles, one will find him/herself walking in compromise. Guinness and Seel concur that Christians compromise in extremes – *"Some, at*

---
[17] Guiness and Seel, p. 29.

the one extreme, are neither of the world nor in it, and therefore are isolated. Others, at the other extreme, are both in the world and of it, and therefore are compromised."[18]

With the immergence of television evangelism in the early 70s with Oral Roberts, Billy Graham, Pat Robertson, Rex Humbard, and others, the Pentecostal movement was hitting the airwaves with the gospel being preached in millions of households across America.

The 80s was a decade marked by ministers of the gospel falling prey to carnality, complacency, and compromise – …lusts of the flesh, lust of the eyes and the pride of life…(1

---

[18] *Ibid,* p. 165.

John 2:16). Within this era, the Pentecostal movement was about to encounter devastating scandals that would shake Christiandom. Televangelist and former president of PTL Ministries, Jim Bakker was exposed for repeated sexual indiscretions, fraud, and conspiracy. The press and media did not spare Jim Bakker any mercy when reporting on the multitude of transgressions that caused total embarrassment and eventual incarceration. It was reported that:

> The IRS revoked the PTL's tax-exempt status for owing $65 million in back taxes; illegally taking $4 million in bonuses from PTL funds, defrauding at least 150,000 contributors to the PTL, mail fraud, tax evasion and defrauding the thousands of 'lifetime partners' who bought memberships to Heritage USA, and conspiring to create and continue to lead a lavish and extravagant lifestyles. Bakker was

> found guilty on 24 counts of fraud and conspiracy and sentenced to 45 years in jail and fined $500,000.[19]

On February 21, 1988, another television evangelist, Jimmy Swaggart publicly confessed to "moral failure" (consorting with a prostitute) in front of a congregation of 7,000 in Baton Rouge, Louisiana and resigned from ministry.[20] Jimmy Swaggart offered no excuses for his sin, but rather, repented openly to God and asked for forgiveness. It was further reported by *Charisma News Service*, that Jimmy Swaggart was named in a lawsuit for copyright infringement and plagiarism of Finis Jennings Dake's publications for "wrongfully taking and using plaintiff's

---

[19] Group Watch. *Praise The Lord Ministry*. namebase.org
[20] On This Day.
news.bbc.co.uk/onthisday/hi/dates/stories/february/21

proprietary works for their own benefit and profit."[21]

The tragedy of carnality, complacency, and compromise does not end here but is relentless in flaunting its ugly heads in the lives of men and woman of God. The war is on, but Christians are quickly losing this battle because the prince of this world, Satan is deceiving the very elect. The enemy is tempting the saints of God just like he tempted Jesus. So, the saints must speak the Word of God and use it in the arsenal against the attack of the enemy since "the weapons of our warfare are not carnal, but mighty through God to the pulling down of

---

[21] Charismanews.com, *Jimmy Swaggart Sued For Alleged Copyright Wrongs,* 2001.

strongholds; Casting down imaginations, and every high thing that exalteth itself against the knowledge of God, and bringing into captivity every thought to the obedience of Christ" (2 Corinthians 10:4, 5).

The decade of the 90s shifted national attention to Rev. Henry Lyons, president of the National Baptist Convention. In the March 15, 1999 edition of Charisma News Service, the article reported that:

> The Rev. Henry Lyons, convicted of swindling $4 million as head of the National Baptist Convention U.S.A. will announce his resignation during a television interview tonight on ABC-TV. He was convicted of grand theft for stealing nearly $250,000 donated by the Anti-Defamation League of B'Nai B'rith to rebuild burned black churches in the South.

> Lyons faces 54 charges of extortion, tax evasion, conspiracy and fraud.[22]

Henry Lyons was also found guilty of having an adulterous affair which brought much shame and reproach to his home, church, community, and Christiandom. Too many Christians enjoy "sin for a season" and become entwined in a deceptive web believing that all is well. However, it is written, "What shall we say then? Shall we continue in sin, that grace may abound? God forbid. How shall we, that are dead to sin, live any longer therein?" (Romans 6:1,2). Rev. Lyons was incarcerated for his crimes.

---

[22] Charismanews.com, *Embattled National Baptist President, Henry Lyons, Expected To Resign Tonight.* March 15, 1999.

In an article entitled, "Securities Regulators Warn Faith-based Scams 'Larger and More Sophisticated' was printed in Charisma News Service, suggested that "more money is stolen in the name of God than in any other way."[23] Scams have been commonly linked to low-life hustlers and the like. However, it's tragic when ministers from the house of God are ring leaders in a scam to swindle money from God's people. Accordingly, Gerald Payne, founder of Greater Ministries International Church was convicted of conspiracy, religious fraud, and money laundering that paid established investors with money from recent

---

[23] Charismanews.com, *Securities Regulators Warn Faith-based Scams 'Larger and More Sophisticated'*. August 7, 2001.

investors."[24] Carnality has crept so subtly into the hearts and minds of Christians that complacency has settled in and compromise has become part of the moral fiber. The <u>Amplified</u> version of 2 Timothy 3:2 states:

> For people will be lovers of self and [utterly] self-centered, lovers of money and aroused by an inordinate [greedy] desire for wealth, proud and arrogant and contemptuous boasters. They will be abusive (blasphemous, scoffing), disobedient to parents, ungrateful, unholy and profane.

The accuser of the brethren has been given too much ammunition to denounce believers before Jesus. **Thank God for Jesus** who declares the believer justified and righteous before God.

---

[24] *Ibid.*

While saints of God are covered by the blood of Jesus, believers cannot be ignorant of the signs of the times. The Bible reads, "Now the Spirit speaketh expressly, that in the latter times some shall depart from the faith, giving heed to seducing spirits, and doctrines of devils; Speaking lies in hypocrisy; having their conscience seared with a hot iron" (1 Timothy 4:1, 2).

With the turn of a new millennium, you would think that Christians would have taken heed of fellow believers who were caught in sin. Why would anyone jeopardize failing in ministry, losing everything, surrendering to public humiliation and living in captivity? Or, even worse, falling into the hands of an angry God?

The prophet Jeremiah tells his reader in 48:10, "Cursed be he that doeth the work of the LORD deceitfully..." Regardless of repeated warnings and inherent penalties for lawbreakers in the Bible as well as in the secular world, some Christians are blinded by the hand of the enemy, believing that they are too clever to be caught.

Satan is a master deceiver who contorts biblical truths to confound the believer. In the Prophecy Study Bible, authored by John C. Hagee, nine types of deception are discussed including: 1) Religious 2) Doctrinal 3) Ethical 4) Moral 5) Intellectual 6) Fanatical 7) Mystical 8)

Sexual and 9) Spiritual.[25] The enemy attacks the body of Christ in all the above mentioned areas with the intent to obliterate the kingdom of God. Be that as it may, Satan is a defeated foe and the Lord has a remnant that will fulfill His divine will and reign on earth victoriously!

The new millennium brought more scandals, cover-ups, and shame to the household of faith. According to Christianity Today, cases were reported in New York, Los Angeles, Connecticut, Maine, Ohio, Pennsylvania and many other places around the country on sexual abuse of children and

---

[25] John C. Hagee, Prophesy Study Bible, *"What Is the Day of Deception?"* (Nashville, TN: Thomas Nelson Publishers, 1997), pp. 1186, 1187.

adolescents by Roman Catholic clergy.[26] It was further alleged that archbishops of various dioceses are protecting known pedophile priests whereby many parishioners have lost faith in leadership and have demanded prompt resignations.[27] These acts of disobedience resulted in costly litigation and multimillion dollar settlements leaving victims scarred with potentially long term mental, physical, and emotional damage. Although the Roman Catholic church is being scrutinized and criticized for such appalling misconduct, other denominations have been accused of the same

---

[26] Ted Olsen and Todd Hertz, *"How the Cleary Sexual Abuse Scandal Affects Evangelical Churches"* Christianity Today.com (March 2002).
[27] *Ibid.*

behavior; however, it has been contained and resolved within the particular church. Scandals of this nature have a damaging impact on how the "world" views Christianity, leadership, and laity alike. It appears that Christians are *practicing* the same sins as people "in the world" which would classify many believers as hypocrites!

In an article written by Andy Butcher, entitled, *"Televangelist Decries Prosperity Message 'Deception'*, statements were made concerning ministers of the gospel preaching on prosperity in an attempt to "short-circuit a supernatural response from God," which reads:

> Although the principle of sowing and reaping is an important aspect of giving, it has been distorted. One of

> the huge deceptions in some personal prosperity teaching is the notion that everybody is going to have a big house, big car or big income. . . It questions whether prosperity teaching is 'not simply a means of excusing the lifestyle and assuaging the consciences of wealthy Christians,' and observes the image of the prosperous, high-profile charismatic leader...can easily replace Christ as the object of adulation and imitation.[28]

As joint-heirs with Christ, believers are entitled to the promises of God. However, you must adhere to specific biblical principles by putting things in proper perspective, "But seek ye **first** the kingdom of God, and his righteousness; and all these things shall be added unto you" (Matthew 6:33). Proverbs 28:13 clearly states, "He that covereth his sins

---

[28] Andy Butcher, *Charismanews.com*, "Televangelist Decries Prosperity Message 'Deception' (April 2003).

shall **not** prosper; but whoso confesseth and forsaketh them shall have mercy." The Holy Scriptures also inform the reader that, "For you always have the poor among you, but you will not always have Me" (Matthew 26:11 AMP). It is imperative that ministers teach biblical truths versus religion, church doctrine, and hype, because believers will be led astray from God and suffer a spiritual demise.

Losing focus on kingdom building for God's glory is the most probable cause for saints falling into "divers temptations" in pursuit of prosperity. Therefore, ministers of the gospel must be careful when teaching biblical principles regarding prosperity and avoid using catchy clichés like "Name it and claim it", speak those things which are not as though they "were" and "You can't beat God at giving." God desires the best for His people and His Word declares, "Beloved, I wish above all things that thou mayest prosper and be in health, even as thy soul prospereth" (3 John 2). Inasmuch as God desires good health and wealth for His children, believers must "Love not the world, neither the things that are in the world...For all that is in the world – the lust of the flesh [craving for sensual gratification] and the lust of the eyes [greedy longings of the mind] and the pride of life [assurance in one's own resources or in the stability of earthly things] – these do not come from the Father, but are from the world [itself]" (1 John 2:15, 16 AMP).

Unfortunately, more and more cases of infidelity among Christian leaders are being exposed across all denominations. It has become so prevalent that many church communities have witnessed the devastating affects of this horrific lust demon (e.g., broken families, broken covenants between husband and wife, divisions in the church, pastoral resignations, mistrust, suspicion, gossip, lies, wavering faith, etc.). The adversary is playing for keeps in an attempt to take as many believers or nonbelievers with him to suffer torment in eternal death. Therefore, believers are admonished to stop "playing church" and "Seek ye the Lord while he may be found, call ye upon him while he is near: Let the wicked forsake his way, and the unrighteous man his thoughts: and let him return unto the LORD, and he will have mercy upon him; and to our God, for he will abundantly pardon" (Isaiah 55:6, 7); or forfeit an everlasting life of peace and joy.

Believers must understand that the church is a place to make a spiritual deposit of praise and worship to the Lord. This means "an action" is required from the Lord by the believer to participate and not spectate. Be that as it may, some Christians as well as unbelievers sit back and wait for someone to entertain them in the way the world entertains its own.

> Many today believe that church meetings should entertain unbelievers for the purpose of

> creating a good experience that will make Christ more palatable to them...They say the church must adopt new methods and innovative programs to grab people on the level where they live.[29]

Many Christians have heard and supported this concept. Some have expressed the following: "The youth are not going to get saved by hymns anymore." "We have to bring gospel rap into the church because that is the music youth understand." It's okay if they dance the same way at a party in the church. After all, they changed partners. Now they are dancing for Jesus." With this mindset, the church is living a self-fulfilling tragedy of compromise.

---

[29] Ernest D. Pickering, *The Tragedy of Compromise*. (Greenville, South Carolina: Bob Jones University Press, 1994), p. 133.

CHAPTER FOUR

THE CHRISTIAN VOICE – THE SURVEY

That the God of our Lord Jesus Christ, the Father of glory, may give unto you the spirit of wisdom and revelation in the knowledge of him: The eyes of your understanding being enlightened; that ye may know what is the hope of his calling, and what the riches of the glory of his inheritance in the saints.
(Ephesians 1:17,18 KJV)

A Christian Survey was randomly distributed to two hundred twenty-five Christians in the Tampa Bay area in Florida (Tampa,

Clearwater and St. Petersburg). The survey provided anonymity while gender, denomination, membership and leadership status was identified. A total of twenty statements required a response of **agree** or **disagree**. The responses were indicative of the Christians' beliefs and lifestyles.

The Survey

The data was collected, compiled, and analyzed. The results were compelling and will be closely examined according to the Word of God as it relates to the twenty survey statements.

<u>Statement #1</u> – Holy means "pure, sacred"…Holiness means being totally devoted or dedicated to God.

> [Earnestly] remember the Sabbath day, to keep it holy (withdrawn from common employment and dedicated to God). Exodus 20:8 AMP.

Statement #2 – God requires Christians to live holy because He is holy.

> Sanctify yourselves therefore, and be ye holy: for I am the LORD your God. Leviticus 20:7

> But as he which hath called you is holy, so be ye holy in all manner of conversation. Because it is written, Be ye holy; for I am holy. 1 Peter 1:15, 16.

> For God hath not called us unto uncleanness, but unto holiness. 1 Thessalonians 4:7.

Statement #3 – The concept of "holiness" is taught at my church.

> For [our earthly fathers] disciplined us and we yielded [to them] and respected [them for training us]. Shall we not much more cheerfully submit to the Father of spirits and so [truly] live? Hebrews 12:10 AMP

And to the genealogy of all their little ones, their wives, and their sons, and their daughters, through all the congregation: for their set office they sanctified themselves in holiness. 2 Chronicles 31:18

Statement #4 – The thought of living holy is too difficult – after all, I'm only human.

And she said unto her husband, Behold now, I perceive that this is an holy man of God, which passeth by us continually. 2 Kings. 4:9

Having therefore these promises, dearly beloved, let us cleanse ourselves from all filthiness of the flesh and spirit, perfecting holiness in the fear of God. 2 Corinthians 7:1

According as he hath chosen us in him before the foundation of the world, that we should be holy and without blame before him in love. Ephesians 1:4

I beseech you therefore, brethren, by the mercies of God, that ye present your bodies a living sacrifice, holy, acceptable unto God, which is your reasonable service. Romans 12:1

Statement #5 – There is nothing wrong with drinking alcoholic beverages at social functions or simply to unwind after a long rough day.

> Woe unto them that rise up early in the morning, that they may follow strong drink; that continue until night, till wine inflame them! Isaiah 5:11

> It is good neither to eat flesh, nor to drink wine, nor any thing whereby thy brother stumbleth, or is offended, or is made weak. Romans 14:21

> Wine is a mocker and beer a brawler; whoever is led astray by them is not wise. Proverbs 20:1 NIV

> Drink no longer water, but use a little wine for they stomach's sake and thine often infirmities. 1 Timothy 5:23

> These also reel with wine and staffer with strong drink; the priest and the prophet reel with strong drink, they are confused with wine, they stagger with strong drink; they err in vision, they stumble in giving judgment. Isaiah 28:7 NRSV

Statement #6 – Cursing every now and then is acceptable especially when provoked.

> Out of the same mouth proceedeth blessing and cursing. My brethren, these things ought not so to be. James 3:10
>
> For the sin of their mouth and the words of their lips let them even be taken in their pride: and for cursing and lying which they speak. Psalm 59:12
>
> You shall not misuse the name of the LORD your God, for the LORD will not hold anyone guiltless who misuses his name. Exodus 20:7 NIV
>
> But above all things, my brethren, swear not, neither by heaven, neither by the earth, neither by any other oath: but let your yea be yea; and your nay, nay; lest ye fall into condemnation. James 5:12

Statement #7 – Everyone gossips – so it's okay to listen as long as I don't contribute.

> An evildoer gives heed to wicked lips; and a liar listens to a mischievous tongue. Proverbs 17:4 AMP

> But I say unto you, That every idle word that men shall speak, they shall give account thereof in the day of judgment. For by thy words thou shalt be justified, and by thy words thou shalt be condemned. Matthew 12:36, 37

> Beloved, believe not every spirit, but try the spirits whether they are of God: because many false prophets are gone out into the world. 1 John 4:1

Statement #8 – A man/woman of God can wear any type of clothing regardless of how revealing, seductive or gangster-looking it might be.

> My son, if sinners entice thee, consent thou not. Proverbs 1:10

> The righteous is more excellent than his neighbour: but the way of the wicked seduceth them. Proverbs 12:26

> Now the Spirit speaketh expressly, that in the latter times some shall depart from the faith, given heed to seducing spirits, and doctrines of devils. 1 Timothy 4:1

> The woman shall not wear that which pertaineth unto a man, neither shall a man put on a woman's garment: for all that do so are abomination unto the LORD thy God. Deuteronomy 22:5

> But one is tempted by one's own desire, being lured and enticed by it; then, when that desire has conceived, it gives birth to sin, and that sin, when it is fully grown, gives birth to death. Do not be deceived my beloved. James 1:14-16 NRSV

Statement #9 – It's all right to compromise my Christian principles by any means necessary if it means getting the edge over someone else.

> They feared the LORD, and served their own gods, after the manner of the nations whom they carried away from thence. 2 Kings 17:33

> No one can serve two masters; for either he will hate the one and love the other, or he will stand by and be devoted to the one and despise and be against the other. You cannot serve God and mammon (deceitful riches, money, possessions, or whatever is trusted in). Matthew 6:24 AMP

> For our appeal [in preaching] does not [originate] from delusion or error or impure purpose or motive, nor in fraud or deceit. But just as we have been approved by God to be entrusted with glad tidings (the Gospel), so we speak not to please men but to please God, Who tests our hearts [expecting them to be approved]. 1 Thessalonians 2:3, 4 AMP

Statement #10 – Although Christian are accountable for their actions, those in leadership must lead by example and therefore, must maintain a higher standard of living before God.

> For a bishop must be blameless, as the steward of God; not self-willed, not soon angry, not given to wine, no striker, not given to filthy lucre; But a lover of hospitality, a lover of good men, sober, just, holy, temperate; Holding fast the faithful word as he hath been taught, that he may be able by sound doctrine both to exhort and to convince the gainsayers. Titus 7-9

> Obey your spiritual leaders and submit to them [continually recognizing their authority over you], for they are constantly keeping watch over your souls and guarding your spiritual welfare, as men who will have to render an account [of their trust]. [Do your part to] let them do this with gladness and not with sighing and groaning, for that would not be profitable to you [either]. Hebrews 13:7 AMP

> Where no counsel is, the people fall: but in the multitude of counselors there is safety. Proverbs 11:14

> The God of Israel said, the Rock of Israel spake to me, He that ruleth over men must be just, ruling in the fear of God. 2 Samuel 23:3

Statement #11 – Anointed musicians and gospel artists minister to the heart, mind, soul and spirit of man.

> Let the word of Christ dwell in you richly in all wisdom; teaching and admonishing one another in psalms and hymns and spiritual songs, singing with grace in your hearts to the Lord. Colossians 3:16

As he that taketh away a garment in cold weather, and as vinegar upon nitre, so is he that singeth songs to an heavy heart. Proverbs 25:20

Let our lord now command thy servants, which are before thee, to seek out a man, who is a cunning player on an harp: and it shall come to pass, when the evil spirit from God is upon thee, that he shall play with his hand, and thou shalt be well. 1 Samuel 16:16

It came even to pass, as the trumpeters and singers were as one, to make one sound to be heard in praising and thanking the LORD; and when they lifted up their voice with the trumpets and cymbals and instruments of music, and praised the LORD, saying, For he is good; for his mercy endureth for ever: that then the house was filled with a cloud, even the house of the LORD; So that he priests could not stand to minister by reason of the cloud: for the glory of the LORD had filled the house of God. 2 Chronicles 5:13, 14

Statement #12 – It is acceptable for Christians to frequent sports bars, Mardi gras, the Jerry Springer Show and Ricki Lake Show.

> Blessed is the man that walketh not in the counsel of the ungodly, nor standeth in the way of sinners, nor sitteth in the seat of the scornful. Psalm 1:1

> Be ye not unequally yoked together with unbelievers: for what fellowship hath righteousness with unrighteousness? And what communion hath light with darkness? Wherefore come out from among them, and be ye separate, saith the Lord, and touch not the unclean thing; and I will receive you. 1 Corinthians 6:14, 17

Statement #13 – Homosexuals and lesbians should occupy positions of leadership in the church.

> Wherefore God also gave them up to uncleanness through the lusts of their own hearts, to dishonour their own bodies between themselves: Who changed the truth of God into a lie, and worshipped and served the creature more than the Creator, who is blessed for ever. Amen. For this cause God gave them up unto vile

> affections: for even their women did change the natural use into that which is against nature: And likewise also the men, leaving the natural use of the woman, burned in their lust one toward another; men with men working that which is unseemly, and receiving in themselves that recompense of their error which was meet. Romans 1: 24-27

> Thou shalt not lie with mankind, as with womankind: it is abomination. Leviticus 18:22

> The look on their faces testifies against them; they parade their sin like Sodom; they do not hide it. Woe to them! They have brought disaster upon themselves. Isaiah 3:9 NIV

Statement #14 – The church is primarily a social institution – a place to network verses a place to learn and apply biblical principles to live a victorious life.

> And Jesus went into the temple of God, and cast out all them that sold and bought in the temple, and overthrew the tables of the money-changers, and the seats of them that sold doves, And said unto them, It is written, My house shall be called the

> house of prayer; but ye have made it a den of thieves. Matthew 21:12, 13

> For the love of money is the root of all evil: which wile some coveted after, they have erred from the faith, and pierced themselves through with many sorrows. 1 Timothy 6:10

Statement #15 – Some choirs incorporate choreographed movements while singing that closely resemble secular dance moves.

> Having a form of godliness, but denying the power thereof; from such turn away. 2 Timothy 3:5

Statement #16 – A lot of gospel music has the same beat as classic R&B tunes. The only difference is the lyrics.

> And it came to pass, as soon as he came nigh unto the camp, that he saw the calf, and the dancing: and Moses' anger waxed hot, and he cast the tables out of his hands, and brake them beneath the mount. Exodus 32:19

> Be ye are a chosen generation, a royal priesthood, an **holy** nation, a peculiar people; that ye should shew

forth the praises of him who hath called you **out** of darkness into his marvelous light. 1 Peter 2:9

Statement #17 – If a Christian attends church regularly and faithfully serves on auxiliaries within the church, God wouldn't mind them kicking up their heels on a dance floor to secular music.

> Blessed is the man that walketh not in the counsel of the **ungodly**, nor standeth in the way of sinners, nor sitteth in the seat of the scornful. Psalm 1:1

> So then because thou are lukewarm, and neither cold nor hot, I will spue thee out of my mouth. Revelation 3:16

> Be ye not unequally yoked together with unbelievers: for what fellowship hath righteousness with unrighteousness? And what communion hath light with darkness? 2 Corinthians 6:14

Statement #18 – There is nothing wrong with a Christian getting tattoos as long as the imprints are not symbolic of ungodly images.

> You shall not make any cuttings in your flesh for the dead nor print or tattoo any marks upon you; I am the Lord. Leviticus 19:28 AMP

> Know ye not that ye are the temple of God, and that Spirit of God dwelleth in you? If any man defile the temple of God, him shall God destroy; for the temple of God is holy, which temple ye are. 1 Corinthians 3:16

Statement #19 – Dipping and dabbing in lusts of the flesh will hinder a Christian's relationship with God.

> Watch and pray, that ye enter not into temptation: the spirit indeed is willing, but the flesh is weak. Matthew 26:41

> This I say then, Walk in the Spirit, and ye shall not fulfill the lust of the flesh. For the flesh lusteth against the Spirit, and the Spirit against the flesh: and these are contrary the one to the other: so that ye cannot do the things that ye would. Galatians 5:16, 17

> So then they that are in the flesh cannot please God. Romans 8:8

> For I know that in me (that is, in my flesh,) dwelleth no good thing: for to will is present with me; but how to perform that which is good I find not. For the good that I would I do not: but the evil which I would not, that I do. Romans 7:18, 19

Statement #20 – It is fairly easy to pick a Christian out of a crowd because (s)he walks and talks differently from "the crowd."

> But ye are a chosen generation, a royal priesthood, an holy nation, a peculiar people; that ye should show forth the praises of him who hath called you out of darkness into his marvelous light. 1 Peter 2:9

> Let your light so shine before men, that they may see your good works, and glorify your Father which is in heaven. Matthew 5:16

A total of fifty-one questions were left unanswered which consisted of pastors, elders, deacons, deaconesses, teachers, and lay people. Since the random samples concealed the identities of the participants, I cannot say with any degree of certainty as to the underlying reasons for these missing responses. I could only surmise that the respondents: were unsure of the "biblically correct" answer; did not want to appear ignorant of Godly principles; did not choose to reveal their understanding of the truth; and/or were clueless.

The results of the Christian Survey as well as the writer's other findings provide striking evidence which supports the title of this book – that the church is dying spiritually due to carnality, complacency, and compromise.

According to the survey, ninety-six percent of the Christian church is teaching about holiness, while approximately thirteen percent have not gravitated towards or embraced this Godly principle.

The social scene revealed that although most respondents would not frequent sports bars, Mardi gras, the Ricki Lake Show or Jerry Springer Show, twenty-five percent agreed to partaking in alcoholic beverages at social functions, and sixteen percent had no problem with kicking up their heels on a dance floor to secular music.

Regarding appropriate attire for men and women of God, ten percent agreed that gangster-looking, revealing or seductive clothing was acceptable. Additionally, twenty-three percent agreed with getting tattoos.

Interestingly, eleven percent of the respondents agreed that homosexuals and lesbians should occupy positions of leadership in the church.

According to the data, eighty-four percent of the respondents agreed that a lot of gospel music has the same beat as classic R&B tunes and eighty percent agreed that choirs incorporate choreographed movements with singing that closely resembles secular dances moves.

If forty-two percent of the respondents view the church primarily as a social institution, imagine what the perception is from those on the outside? "Gossip – everyone gossips – so it's okay to *listen* as long as I don't contribute," was the response of seventeen percent of the participants. The data further indicated that forty-one percent of the respondents found it difficult to pick a Christian out of a crowd because their walk and talk is similar to "the crowd."

Thirteen percent of the respondents disagreed that leadership should lead by example and therefore, maintain a higher standard of living before God.

Five percent agreed that it is all right to **compromise** Christian principles by any means necessary such as cussing, which was indicated by seven percent of the respondents.

Finally, twenty-one percent of the respondents actually disagreed that dipping and dabbing in lusts of the flesh *will* hinder a Christian's relationship with God.

CONCLUSION

"...in the last days perilous times shall come. For men shall be lovers of their own selves, covetous, boasters, proud, blasphemers, disobedient to parents, unthankful, unholy. Traitors, heady, highminded, lovers of pleasures more than lovers of God; Having a form of godliness, but denying the power thereof: from such turn away. For of this sort are they which creep into houses, and lead captive silly women laden with sins, led away with divers lusts, Ever learning, and never able to come to the knowledge of the truth."
(2 Timothy 3:2, 4-7)

Undoubtedly, the Christian church is suffering from some serious problems. This book has uncovered how men and women of

God are infested with spiritual infirmities, rebellion, and disobedience to the Word of God. Consequently, these incidences are not limited to the confines of this book. There is a myriad of unreported spiritual disasters involving both men and women of God that have fallen into the same snares of the enemy as those documented in this book. Many local church communities across the nation can attest to this dilemma and the only reason it is not publicized in the media is because their names are usually infamous. If Christians continue to conceal their spiritual infirmities without repentance, and refuse to seek God's true healing and deliverance power, the human soul will erode and result in spiritual demise.

Christians must make a conscious decision to follow Christ and stop following the world by imitating things of the world instead of things of God; concentrating on more earthly, temporal things rather than on eternal things and; entering into the house of the Lord waiting to be entertained rather than offering a spirit of thanksgiving and worship. We must understand that sin only lasts for a season, but its lethal poison can cause eternal damage. So, don't get tricked into believing that getting **by** with sin means getting **away** because "…the wages of sin is death…" (Romans 6:23).

The Christian church must abandon all ideologies of manipulation, self-indulgence, and compromise because time is quickly running out before Jesus returns.

While some of the response percentages appeared low between ten to twenty-five percent, we must not lose sight on these numbers and become nonchalant. If one bad apple can spoil a whole bunch, how much more can ten to twenty-five percent of carnal, complacent, and compromising Christians infect a nation? The Word of God states in Romans 12:1,2:

> I beseech you therefore, brethren, by the mercies of God, that ye present your bodies a living sacrifice, holy, acceptable unto God, which is your reasonable service. And be **not** conformed to this world; but be ye transformed by the renewing of your mind, that ye may prove what is that good, and acceptable, and perfect will of God.

We must pray without ceasing and allow God to operate on our heart and allow the Holy Spirit to guide us into safe waters and the truth. Believers can no longer risk looking to the left or to the right (at their brethren, sister, leaders, etc.), because man will falter and possibly cause another to stumble. As such, believers must look to Jesus who is the author and finisher of their faith.

"Now unto him that is able to do exceeding abundantly above all that we ask or think, according to the power that worketh in us."
(Ephesians 3:20)

BIBLIOGRAPHY

Butcher, Andy. "Televangelist Decries Prosperity Message 'Deception'. "*Charismanews.com* (April 2003).

"Coverups Prompt Demands for Resignation." *ChristianityToday.com* 46 (May 2002)

"Embattled National Baptist President, Henry Lyons, Expected to Resign Tonight." *Charismanews.com* (March 1999).

Fager, Chuck. "Scam Hits Black Churches." *ChristianityToday.com* 46 (December 2002): 20.

GroupWatch. "Jimmy Swaggart Ministries." *Namebase.org* (January 1989).

_____. "Praise The Lord Ministry." *Namebase.org* (May 1990).

Guinness, Os and John Seel. *No God But God.* Chicago, Illinois: Moody Press, 1992.

Hagee, John C. *Prophesy Study Bible*. Nashville, TN: Thomas Nelson Publishers, 1997.

Ilumina Encyclopedia, 2d ed., s.v. "Holiness, Holy" [CD-ROM] (Tyndale House Publishers, 2002).

_____. Holiness of God.

"Jimmy Swaggart Sued For Alleged Copyright Wrongs." *Charismanews.com* (June 2001).

King James/Amplified Parallel Bible. Grand Rapids, MI: Zondervan Publishing House, 1995.

Lahaye, Tim. *Revelation Unveiled*: Revised Edition. Grand Rapids, Michigan: Zondervan Publishing House, 1999.

The Layman's Parallel Bible. Grand Rapids, MI: Zondervan Publishing House, 1991.

The Open Bible Expanded Edition, New King James Version. Nashville, Tennessee: Thomas Nelson Publishers, 1985.

"Laodicea." *Ourfatherlutheran.net* (November 1998).

Marshall, Howard I., A.R. Millard, A.R., Packer, J.I. and Wiseman, D.J. *The New Bible Dictionary*, Downers Grove, Illinois: Intervarsity Press, 1999.

Olford, Stephen. *The Way of Holiness*. Wheaton, Illinois: Crossway Books, 1998.

Olsen, Ted and Todd Hertz. *How the Clergy Sexual Abuse Scandal Affects Evangelical Churches*. *ChristianityToday.com* (March 2002).

"On This Day." *news.bbc.co.uk/on this day* (February 1988).

"Pastor's 'Indiscretion' Forces Resignation." *Charismanews.com* (February 2002).

Pickering, Ernest D. *The Tragedy of Compromise – The Origin and Impact of the New Evangelicalism*. Greenville, South Carolina: Bob Jones University Press, 1994.

Revell, Fleming H. *The Revell Bible Dictionary*. Grand Rapids, MI: Baker Book House Company, 1994.

"Securities Regulators Warn Faith-based Scams 'Larger And More Sophisticated' ". *Charismanews.com* (August 2001).

Walvoord, John F. *The Revelation of Jesus Christ*. Chicago, IL: Moody Press, 1989.

Webster's Ninth New Collegiate Dictionary. Springfield, Massachusetts: Merriam-Webster Publishers, 1984.

ABOUT THE AUTHOR

Dr. Darlene Townsend is a native New Yorker who truly reverences the awesomeness of the Almighty God. She was employed full-time as the director of state and federally funded programs at the Greater Allen A.M.E. Cathedral of New York where the Rev. Dr. Floyd H. Flake was her pastor.

In her latter years in New York, the Lord shifted her to a deliverance ministry where her spiritual father was Pastor John H. Boyd, Sr. While there, she became the full-time administrator to the assistant pastor, John H. Boyd, II, special assistant to the Dean of New Greater Bethel Bible Institute, and the liaison for Shekinah International (the former gospel recording company for Juanita Bynum and Valerie Boyd).

For many years, Dr. Townsend served faithfully in both ministries in various capacities including music, youth, auxiliaries, and leadership.

She received her secular education from Howard University and Miami

University, where she earned a Bachelor of Science and Master of Arts degrees, respectively. Her theological studies resulted in a Bachelor's degree from Vision International University, a Masters and Doctorate of Ministry in Theology from Life Christian University.

Throughout her years of advanced learning, Dr. Townsend walked in the Word and *"studied to show herself approved unto God, a workman that needeth not to be ashamed, rightly dividing the word of truth"* (2 Tim. 2:15). As such, she was the recipient of numerous honors and awards for her outstanding achievement in biblical studies.

Dr. Townsend is also a former Professor of Christian Education and English Composition who is dedicated to writing with excellence! Her writings are the true inspiration of the Holy Spirit – for without His leading, these pages would be blank.

She is a yielded vessel with multi-faceted gifts and talents who is available for the Master's use when He calls for teaching, preaching, editing, armorbearer training, workshop facilitating, prophetic dancing, and anything additional He desires.

Proof

Made in the USA
Charleston, SC
29 October 2010